D1035544

Copyright © 2017 by Herald Entertainment, Inc., McKinney, TX
All Rights Reserved
Illustrations by Herald Entertainment, Inc.
Visit our Brother Francis series website at: www.brotherfrancis.com
Printed in China
First Printing: August 2017
ISBN: 978-1-939182-75-3

Brother Francis

The Angel God Gave Me

A book about our Guardian Angels

God loves
me. When
I was born,
He gave me
an angel to
be with me
always.

The angel God gave me is my Guardian Angel. Just like Jesus, my Guardian Angel loves me too!

This special angel watches over me day and night. He helps take care of me.

My Guardian Angel guards me. He helps to keep me safe.

(Psalm 91:11)

4

My Guardian
Angel is my very
special friend.

5

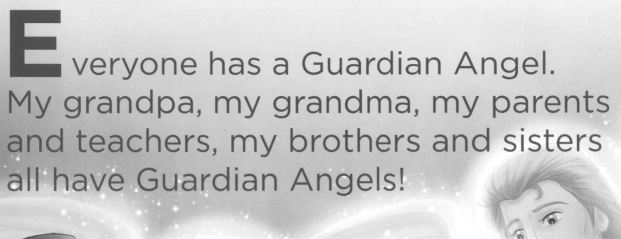

E veryone has a Guardian Angel.
My grandpa, my grandma, my parents
and teachers, my brothers and sisters
all have Guardian Angels!

We cannot see them, but Guardian Angels are always near.

7

My Guardian Angel watches over me when I am awake and when I am asleep.

8

He is with me when I am walking and when I am running.

He is always there when I am playing and when I am working.

9

What else does
my Guardian Angel do?

My Guardian Angel
encourages me to do
good things.

When I remember to stop and thank God for my blessings, my Guardian Angel is so happy!

When I do good things for others, my Guardian Angel is happy too!

When I am tempted to do something wrong, my Guardian Angel reminds me to be good.

13

If ever I am afraid, my Guardian Angel helps me to remember that God is with me.

When we come to God, our Guardian Angel rejoices!

My Guardian Angel is
my special friend!

A Poem About My Guardian Angel

My Guardian Angel watches over me both day & night.

He walks so close beside me that I am never out of sight.

Though I may never see him,
I know that he is here.

My angel helps me trust in God
if ever I feel fear.

He sees the way before me,
and points to guide my way.
He helps me stay quite close to
God and not to go astray.

If ever I feel sad, discouraged or alone, my special friend reminds me that God is on His throne.

20

He tells me God is listening, reminding me to pray. He's happy when I'm faithful and stay within God's way.

21

He knows my every deed, nothing's hidden from his view. All the things I've done, both good and bad, he knows about those too!

22

He always stays beside me, he keeps me company.
My angel is a special friend and a gift from God for me.

23

If ever you feel all alone, here's what I recommend: Remember your Guardian Angel, your very special friend!

24

A Prayer to My Guardian Angel

Angel of God
My guardian dear
To whom His love
Commits me here
Ever this day
Be at my side
To light and guard
To rule and guide.

Amen.

For more books like this one, visit:
www.brotherfrancis.com